Rumble, Boom!

A Book About Thunderstorms

by Rick Thomas
illustrated by Denise Shea

Content Adviser: Daniel Dix, Senior Meteorologist,
The Weather Channel

Reading Adviser: Susan Kesselring, M.A., Literacy Educator,
Rosemount-Apple Valley-Eagan (Minnesota) School District

PICTURE WINDOW BOOKS
Minneapolis, Minnesota

Managing Editor: Catherine Neitge
Creative Director: Terri Foley
Art Director: Keith Griffin
Editor: Patricia Stockland
Designer: Nathan Gassman
Page production: Picture Window Books
The illustrations in this book were prepared digitally.

Picture Window Books
5115 Excelsior Boulevard
Suite 232
Minneapolis, MN 55416
877-845-8392
www.picturewindowbooks.com

Printed in the
United States of America.

**Library of Congress
Cataloging-in-Publication Data**
Thomas, Rick, 1954-
   Rumble, boom! : a book about thunderstorms
/ by Rick Thomas ; illustrated by Denise Shea.
      p. cm. — (Amazing science)
      Includes bibliographical references and index.
      ISBN 1-4048-0929-5 (hardcover)
         1. Thunderstorms—Juvenile literature. I. Shea, Denise,
         ill. II. Title. III. Series.

      QC968.2.T46 2005
      551.55'4—dc22

      2004023916

Table of Contents

A Thunderstorm Forms 6

Downdrafts 8

Storm Cells and Supercells 10

Electric Energy 12

Thunder and Lightning 14

Squall Lines and Hail 16

Wind Bursts 18

Stormy Planet 20

Surviving a Thunderstorm 22

Extreme Storm Extras 23

Glossary 23

To Learn More 24

Index 24

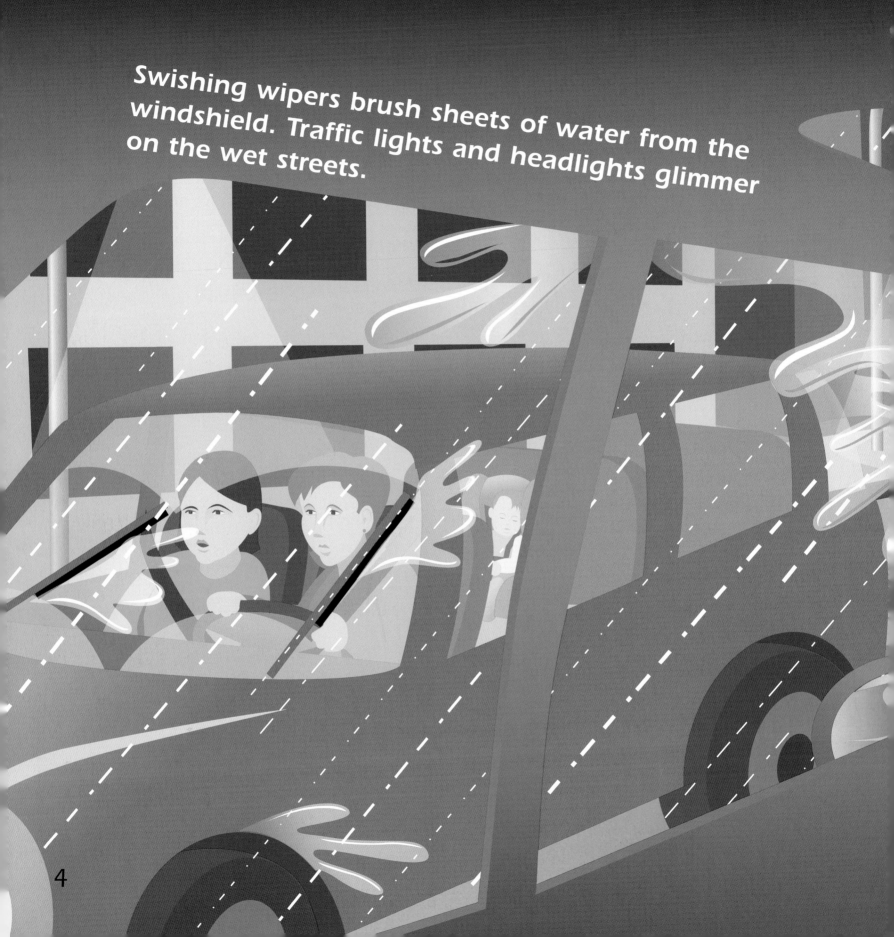

Swishing wipers brush sheets of water from the windshield. Traffic lights and headlights glimmer on the wet streets.

Overhead, dark clouds rush and rumble.
Lightning flashes like a gigantic camera.

Your are caught in a thunderstorm.

A Thunderstorm Forms

Most thunderstorms form during the day, when the air is warmed by the sun. Air is full of water vapor. As air warms, it rises into the sky. The water vapor also rises higher and higher.

When water vapor rises through the air, it mixes with dust. Vapor and dust form clouds. Some clouds can grow into giant shapes with wide, flat tops. These clouds are called anvil clouds.

Downdrafts

Anvil clouds mean rain is on the way.
Watch them pile up, growing thick
and dark. The clouds are full of millions
of water droplets. They block out
the sunlight.

The droplets grow in size as they cool off. They stop rising. Some of the drops fall back to the ground as rain. They carry cool air with them. Cool air rushing downward from the sky is called a downdraft.

Storm Cells and Supercells

Falling cold air and rising warm air form a storm cell. A thunderstorm is made of one or more cells. When the water droplets in the storm cloud turn into rain, the drops fall away. The cell grows smaller and smaller. The storm begins to die. Most thunderstorms last about 30 minutes.

Sometimes, wind and extra cold air can make a cell grow even bigger. Groups of cells swirl and gather together, building into one supercell thunderstorm. Supercells can last for hours. These storms are full of dangerous winds, pouring rain, and thunder and lightning.

11

Electric Energy

Thunderstorms carry electricity. The rising and falling air within a storm cloud builds up a powerful electric charge. The charge carries more than 300,000 volts of electricity per foot. Only 12 volts are needed to run your car engine. So, a thunderstorm holds enough energy to run a million cars.

13

Thunder and Lightning

Thunder is the sound of the heated air rising and expanding at super speed. This air can travel more than 1,000 feet per second. That's four times faster than the world's fastest car.

14

Lightning flashes. A single bolt of lightning can make the air in its path five times hotter than the surface of the sun. Lightning can strike buildings and power poles. It can split trees, melt telephone wires, and set fire to grass.

Squall Lines and Hail

Thunderstorms can travel together. Their edges form a single, long wall of menacing clouds called a squall line. This line can stretch 100 miles across the sky.

Squall lines bring heavy rain. If rain droplets fall through extremely cold air, the drops freeze and turn into hail. Hail can break windows, dent cars, and damage crops.

Wind Bursts

Cold downdrafts pick up speed as they head toward the ground. Some downdrafts bring dangerous bursts of wind. These bursts are sometimes called microbursts.

During most thunderstorms, airplanes can fly above the storm clouds. But strong storms keep many airplanes grounded. A strong microburst might shove against a plane's wings and cause the airplane to lose control.

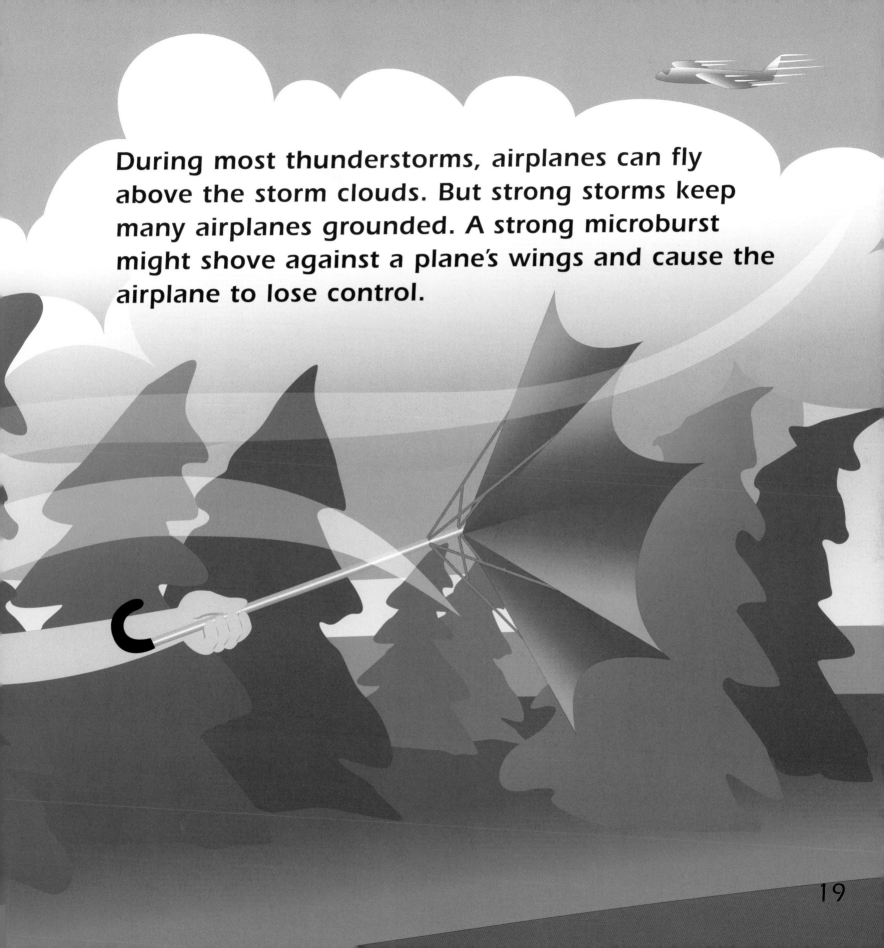

Stormy Planet

Thunderstorms bring lightning strikes, powerful winds, and enough rain to cause flash floods.

Every day, between 1,500 and 2,000 thunderstorms rumble and boom somewhere on Earth. Every minute, 6,000 lightning bolts flash.

Every hour, storms build up, weaken, and die. Thunder and lightning fade away.

Surviving a Thunderstorm

The three biggest dangers from a thunderstorm are lightning strikes, flash floods, and strong winds. If you are caught outside during a thunderstorm, seek shelter. Injury can be avoided by staying indoors and away from windows.

- In a severe electrical storm, turn off or unplug TVs, radios, and computers. Unplug phone lines or cables leading into computer modems. Lightning can travel through wires and into houses.

- Listen to local weather stations on a transistor radio. In cases of flash floods, stay away from low areas, such as ditches, riverbanks, and storm drains.

- If tornadoes or straight-line winds occur, take shelter in basements. If a basement is not available, hide under heavy furniture or in hallways in the middle of a building.

- The 30/30 rule is a good guideline for staying away from lightning. When you see a flash of lightning, begin counting. If you hear thunder before you reach 30, it means the lightning is close by. After the last flash of lightning you see, wait 30 minutes before leaving your shelter.

Extreme Storm Extras

- The average lightning bolt can contain as much energy as a nuclear reactor.

- Lightning can strike up to 10 miles (16 kilometers) away from the storm that produced it. It comes from an anvil cloud and strikes under seemingly blue skies.

- One of the largest hailstones on record came from a supercell thunderstorm that roared through Aurora, Nebraska, in 2003. The hailstone was 7 inches (18 centimeters) across.

- Lightning does not strike just on Earth. Electrical storms have also been observed on Venus, Jupiter, and Saturn.

Glossary

anvil cloud—a storm cloud with a flat, spreading top

downdraft—a column of air that moves rapidly toward the ground

droplets—tiny drops of water or liquid

menacing—scary or threatening

microburst—a severe wind that blasts down from a thunderstorm

vapor—steam or mist

volt—a unit of pressure that measures the force of electricity

To Learn More

At the Library

Bowdish, Lynea. *Thunder Doesn't Scare Me!*
New York: Children's Press, 2001.

Chambers, Catherine. *Thunderstorm.*
Chicago: Heinemann Library, 2002.

Flanagan, Alice K. *Thunder and Lightning.*
Chanhassen, MN: Child's World, 2003.

On the Web

FactHound offers a safe, fun way to find Web sites related to this book. All of the sites on FactHound have been researched by our staff. *www.facthound.com*

1. Visit the FactHound home page.
2. Enter a search word related to this book, or type in this special code: 1404809295
3. Click on the FETCH IT button.

Your trusty FactHound will fetch the best sites for you!

Index

anvil clouds, 7, 8, 23
downdrafts, 9, 18, 23
electricity, 12
flash floods, 20, 22
hail, 17, 23
lightning, 5, 11, 15, 20, 22, 23
squall lines, 16, 17
storm cell, 10, 11
supercell, 11, 23
thunder, 11, 14, 20, 22

Look for all of the books in this series:

Eye of the Storm: A Book About Hurricanes

Flakes and Flurries: A Book About Snow

Gusts and Gales: A Book About Wind

Nature's Fireworks: A Book About Lightning

Rising Waters: A Book About Floods

Rumble, Boom! A Book About Thunderstorms

Shapes in the Sky: A Book About Clouds

Sizzle! A Book About Heat Waves

Splish! Splash! A Book About Rain

Sunshine: A Book About Sunlight

Twisters: A Book About Tornadoes

Whiteout! A Book About Blizzards